THE BROCKHAMPTON LIBRARY

guide to Stain Removal

BROCKHAMPTON PRESS
LONDON

© 1996 Geddes & Grosset Ltd, David Dale House, New Lanark, Scotland.

All rights reserved. No part of this publication may be reproduced, stored in a retrieval system, or transmitted in any form or by any means, electronic, mechanical, photocopying, recording or otherwise, without the prior permission of the copyright holder.

This edition published 1996 by Brockhampton Press, a member of the Hodder Headline PLC Group.

ISBN 1 86019 223 8

Printed and bound in the UK

Contents

Stain Removal — 5
General Tips — 5
Take Action At Once — 6
Identify the Cause of the Stain — 7
Be Prepared — 7
Know Your Fabrics — 8
Spot-Test — 9
Take Care with Chemicals — 10
Be Gentle — 10
Mildest First — 11
Know When to Leave It to the Experts — 12
Removing Stains from Carpets — 12

Stains A-Z — 17
Beer — 17
Beetroot — 18
Bird Droppings — 18
Blood — 19
Butter — 20
Candle Wax — 21
Chewing Gum — 22
Chocolate — 24
Coffee — 25
Cream — 26
Curry — 27
Crayon — 28
Cycle Oil — 28
Deodorant — 29
Dye Runs — 29

Egg	30
Faeces	30
Fizzy Drinks	31
Fruit	32
Glue	33
Grass	34
Gravy	35
Grease	35
Hair Spray	36
Ice Cream	37
Ink	37–40
Jam	40
Ketchup	41
Lipstick	42
Make-up	42
Mildew	43
Milk	44
Mud	45
Nail Varnish	45
Nicotine	46
Paint	47–49
Perspiration	50
Rust	50
Scorch Marks	51
Shoe Polish	51
Tar	52
Tea	52
Urine	53
Vomit	54
Wine	56
Store Cupboard Items for Stain Removal	58

Stain Removal

General Tips

There is nothing more annoying than finding that your new garment, best lounge carpet or favourite tablecloth has been marked in some way. There are certain unavoidable facts about stains. Firstly, stains appear in the most unwelcome places; rarely do they appear on things that are too old to matter—in fact it is almost as if they prefer the new and the delicate! Secondly, they rear their ugly heads in the most prominent places; they almost never appear in places where they can be concealed easily. Thirdly, stains appear at the most inconvenient moments; it is always when time is short that spillages occur and stains appear.

There may be little time to spare to deal with that shoe polish mark on your clothes, and you may find it a nuisance to stop and deal with the spilt wine on the carpet when you should be entertaining your guests, but in order to have the best chance of being able to remove any stain completely, it is important to act as quickly as possible.

Take Action At Once

This is undoubtedly the first rule in the principles and practice of stain removal. The sooner you treat a stain, the less chance it has of setting permanently on whatever material it has marked. Paint spillages provide the obvious example of this rule. Paint is a relatively simple substance to remove from carpets and clothes while it is still wet, but if it is left to dry, it is much harder to remove and can be impossible to get out in some cases.

There are, of course, exceptions to this rule; one exception is mud. Marks that have been left by mud are best left alone until the mud has dried so that any excess can then be brushed off before cleaning.

Identify the Cause of the Stain

If you have not actually seen the mark being made, take a really good look at it and try to be as sure as you can be of what caused it. If you cannot identify the staining agent itself, you should be able to fit it into certain broad categories. Is it greasy? Does it smell of oil, paint or chemicals? Does it smell like some sort of food or drink? Is it dry or wet? Has it penetrated the material completely, or is it just on the surface? What sort of material has it marked?

If you can answer at least some of these questions, you will have a much clearer picture of how to tackle the job.

Be Prepared

It is quite a good idea to keep a few basic items in your store cupboard to assist you in the battle against stains, and a list of these is given at the end of the book.

There are, of course, many proprietary stain removers available on the market, both those that claim to be effective against almost any stain and those that are more specific, targeting smaller groups of stains, such as wine and fruit juice, felt-tip and ballpoint pen. These vary in effectiveness and can be very expensive to use, but one general dry cleaning agent of your own choice can be kept at hand for emergencies. These are available in both liquid and aerosol form. A 'spot remover' for carpets and upholstery in aerosol form can also be quite effective.

The more 'stain-specific' agents can be useful if you are prepared to face the expense, but you may well find that you are able to remove the stain without resorting to these. Many stains can be removed relatively easily, using other, often cheaper, methods, and a few 'stock items' kept to hand will pay their way in the end, especially in a busy household where children, animals and grown-ups are all capable of leaving their mark in various ways!

Know Your Fabrics

There is a very wide variety of materials used to make fabrics for clothing and upholstery and coverings for floors, and these materials are used in many different combinations. Keep a note somewhere of the materials that have been used for all curtains, furniture coverings and carpets in your home. Keep the clothes labels that tell you what they are made from. Some methods of stain removal are not suitable for use on certain materials, such as wool or some man-made fibres. Acetate fibres, for example, can be damaged by methylated spirit, acetone and other solvents. It pays to be cautious!

Spot-Test

Keep small samples of carpet and curtain material if you possibly can, so that you can test them for colour-fastness before you tackle any stain. If you do not have a sample piece of the stained fabric to hand, test your stain-removing solution first on a part of the garment or material where it will not show, such as a seam or the inside of a pocket. Stain removal serves no purpose at all if you remove all the colour from your material in the process!

Take Care with Chemicals

Many of the substances that may be used in the stain-removal process are dangerous if misused. Store all chemicals in a locked cupboard, well out of reach of children. Solvents such as turpentine, white spirit and paint remover are both toxic and highly flammable. Never use such substances near a naked flame, and always work in a well-ventilated area, avoiding inhalation of fumes. Always follow the manufacturer's instructions with great care.

Be Gentle

It is all too tempting to attack a stain with vigorous rubbing and scrubbing, but this really is not the most effective approach, as you run the risk of either spreading the mark, rubbing the staining substance further into the material or worse still, damaging the material itself. No matter how infuriated you are to have found a mark on your favourite garment or your brand-new carpet, do not take out your anger on the stain—it will only react with more stubbornness than before! A gentle dabbing motion and a lot of patience are your best allies in the battle against unsightly marks.

If the material on which you are working is not fixed down, it is often a good idea to start working on the mark from the wrong side of the material, thus pushing the staining substance back out of the material the way it came in. Place a clean pad of absorbent white cloth beneath the stained material as you work, and this will soak up the stain and the excess cleaning solution. Once the pad has become soiled, change it.

Mildest First

If you have more than one option available to you when deciding how to tackle a stain, use the mildest alternative first. Only if that fails should you try anything stronger. The stronger the cleaning substance, the greater the danger of fading or your fabric being damaged. It would be a pity to take drastic action, with drastic results, when something as simple as soap and water and a little patience might have worked!

Know When to Leave It to the Experts

Some fabrics are simply not suitable for do-it-yourself stain removal. Silk, unless it is washable, needs professional care, as do velvet and taffeta. If the label on the garment says 'dry clean only', if the fabric has any sort of special finish, or if you are at all unsure, seek the services of a reliable dry-cleaner as soon as possible. Leather and suede are also best left to the professionals.

Removing Stains from Carpets

If you are able to catch any spillage on carpets immediately, you stand a far better chance of avoiding a difficult or even permanent stain. Don't start rubbing at the mark immediately, however. The first task is to soak up all excess spillage in order to prevent any more from soaking into the fibres. Paper kitchen roll is perfect for this task as it is very absorbent. Place a generous amount over the area of spillage and press down very gently, just enough to allow the spillage to be absorbed by the paper. Change the kitchen roll and repeat this blotting process until you have soaked up as much as you possibly can.

It is better to avoid using soap or detergent if at all possible as these are hard to remove properly from the carpet, so try treating the stain with warm water only first of all. Always work from the outside of the stain towards the inside; in this way you will minimize the danger of spreading the mark. Keep rinsing out the cloth that you are working with and change the water as soon as it becomes discoloured. If you add one or two drops of vinegar or ammonia to the water, this may help to shift the stain.

Blot up excess moisture with kitchen roll as you work; it is important that the area does not become too wet as you risk causing shrinkage and buckling. Wool carpets can take a very long time to dry out and could become mouldy or even start to rot.

If this treatment does not prove to be sufficient, you can then try adding a little liquid detergent to the water. Liquid for washing woollens is quite good to use on carpets.

Great vigilance is required, however, to ensure

that all traces of detergent are rinsed out carefully. Do this by repeatedly applying small amounts of clean water to the area and blotting it up with kitchen roll. Areas of carpet that have been inadequately rinsed will act as a magnet to dirt and grime in the future, so a little extra patience at this point will pay dividends.

Only if you are sure that the gentle approach will not work should you try anything stronger on the carpet.

There are many carpet shampoos and spot-treatments available on the market, but in many cases you will have no need to resort to these. As with detergent, repeated use of such products can cause a build-up of chemicals in the carpet fibres, which can cause the carpet to appear unpleasantly matted and may also attract dirt. Areas of carpet that are subjected to heavy wear and repeated spillages and cleaning will eventually need to be given a thorough all-over cleaning. Steam cleaning is a good way to remove dirt and detergent build-up from carpets. You can hire machinery for steam cleaning from tool-hire merchants and some dry-cleaners, but it is generally much less effort and not much more expensive to get someone in to do this for you.

When buying new carpets, it is always worthwhile considering those that have been pre-treated with stain-repellent. The treatment does not last forever but will certainly help, especially in areas that are likely to be subjected to soiling and spillage. Carpets already *in situ* can be treated with stain-repellent after cleaning, and although it is not cheap to have it done, you may well think that it is worthwhile.

Stains A-Z

Beer

Fresh beer stains will come out without too much problem in a normal wash, preferably using biological powder. Beer spilt on carpets should not leave a stain if the spillage is dealt with immediately. Soak up as much of the spill using absorbent cloths or kitchen roll, then gently work on the mark with warm water and a little detergent.

Clothing marked with dried-in beer stains should be soaked for a while in a solution of warm water and detergent before washing. Some of the darker beers can be more problematic to shift; try rubbing a little glycerine into the stain to loosen it, and leaving it for a while before soaking the article in a solution of warm water and borax. Then rise thoroughly and wash as normal with a biological washing powder.

Beetroot

Beetroot can make a demon stain, but do not despair! If the stain is fresh, dab on a paste made with detergent and lukewarm water. Work this gently through the stain, then immerse the garment in warm water and leave it for half an hour or so to loosen the stain before rinsing it out. Alternatively, dab some lemon juice onto the stain and leave it on for a while, preferably in sunlight, before washing it. If this fails and the fabric is white cotton or linen, you can try soaking it in a household bleach solution, according to the manufacturer's instructions. Rinse thoroughly before washing.

Bird Droppings

These come out quite easily from washable items. Scrape off excess solid matter from the material gently, using the blunt edge of a knife. Soak briefly in warm water and detergent solution before washing as usual.

On non-washable items, a solution of water and household ammonia, used in a ratio of six parts water to one of ammonia, is recommended. Dab this gently on to the mark, then dab on a little white vinegar. When the stain has gone, sponge with a little warm water. Try to avoid over-wetting the fabric.

Blood

Blood is quite easy to remove from most fabrics if the stain is fresh. Soaking the fabric in cold, salty water may be all that is required to remove the mark, but the older the stain, the longer it will have to be soaked, and this is not advisable for woollen fabrics.

If the bloodstain is not fresh, a mixture of one part glycerine to two parts lukewarm water dabbed onto the fabric can help to loosen it, thus avoiding the need for such a lengthy soak. A brief soak in a solution of biological washing powder and water or two tablespoons of borax in one litre of water can also help before the garment is washed.

Non-washable articles of clothing that have been stained with blood may be sponged with cold salty water to which a little ammonia has been added.

On carpets, salt sprinkled onto wet bloodstains will absorb most of the blood. The area should then be gently rubbed with cold, salty water. Remember to work from the outside of the stain inwards.

An alternative is to rub a paste of cornflour and water gently into the stain. When this has dried, brush off the cornflour and repeat as necessary.

Butter

Butter marks will come out without any problem from machine-washable fabrics washed on the normal cycle with a good washing powder.

On non-machine-washable fabrics, talcum powder sprinkled onto the mark and left for twenty-four hours may help to absorb the grease before careful hand-washing. If a greasy mark still remains, try using a little dilute methylated spirit on the stain.

Candle Wax

There is quite a simple trick to remove candle wax drips from carpets and fabric, but it does take a little bit of patience. First of all, wait until the wax has hardened. If you wish, you may want to put small garments in the freezer to speed up the process. Scrape up as much of the lump or lumps of wax as you can, using the blunt edge of a kitchen knife. Place a sheet of blotting paper, or if you have no blotting paper, kitchen roll, over the mark. Heat the iron to a warm setting (not too hot or you risk burning the paper) and press lightly down on the affected area, just briefly. As soon as one area of the paper becomes soaked with the wax, move another bit over the mark and repeat the process. Continue in this manner until no more wax is being taken up by the paper.

On closely woven fabrics, this should be enough to remove all the wax, and you should be able to go on and clean the article as normal. However, on looser-woven fabrics or carpets, some wax may still remain, in which case you can use a little dilute methylated spirit, if you wish, to finish off the process, but take care that you do not fade the colour of the fabric.

Chewing Gum

Why do people dispose of their chewing gum so carelessly? There is nothing more infuriating than treading unwittingly on someone's abandoned gum, only to then trample it into the carpet when you get it home. Children and chewing gum can be a particularly lethal combination; the gum can end up in all sorts of unfortunate places, even in their hair!

It is easiest to remove chewing gum if it is hard. If you find chewing gum stuck to your clothes and the fabric is not a delicate one, don't panic and try to remove it while it is still soft. You risk spreading the gum further over the fabric or pushing it further through. Instead, take off the gummy garment and put it in the freezer until the gum is well hardened. Provided that the gum has not become too enmeshed in the fabric, you should then be able to pick it off quite easily. On carpets, leave the gum to harden as much as possible before attempting to pick it out. You can try holding a piece of ice against the gum to speed up the hardening process.

This treatment will not be successful on any fabric with a pile, such as velvet, as some of the pile is likely to come away with the gum when you pull it off. You can try softening the gum instead with steam and then gently pulling it off bit by bit, but this requires a great deal of patience, and the results may not be entirely successful.

There are products available on the market that are specifically intended for the removal of chewing gum from fabrics. They are certainly worth a try, but read the instructions carefully before you decide to buy, to check whether the product is safe to use on the fabric that you are treating.

If all else fails, a friendly and reliable dry-cleaner may be able to save the day!

The only painless and truly effective means of removing chewing gum from hair has to be cutting it out. Other methods, such as using hand cream to lubricate the gum and help it to slip off the hair, can be quite messy in themselves and more than a squirming child is likely to bear. They also carry the risk of spreading the gum further through the hair.

Chocolate

This is one substance that children are able to spread around very liberally! Luckily, the results are rarely drastic.

Gently scrape up any excess chocolate with the back of a knife or the edge of a spoon. Dabbing the stain with lukewarm water and detergent will help to loosen it before washing. Most modern washing powders will be able to remove the stain completely in a machine wash.

Non-washable fabrics may be sponged gently with lukewarm water, but there may well be a grease mark left, so dry-cleaning is advisable.

Carpets should be rubbed gently with soap and

lukewarm water; take care not to over-wet the area. Rinse with repeated small amounts of water until you are confident the soap has been removed.

You may wish to use a proprietary carpet cleaner, but unless the stain is large, this should not really be necessary.

Coffee

Fresh coffee stains are quite easy to treat. On washable fabrics, a brief soak in detergent and water will be of benefit before washing. Black coffee leaves a darker mark, of course, but should be no less treatable. Fresh black coffee stains on carpets or clothing can be removed with soda water if you have any in the house. Failing that, blotting up excess spillage then dabbing the mark with warm water and a little detergent should be effective, provided that patience is also exercised. When treating carpets, try to use the minimum amount of water necessary for the task.

Older stains on washable items can be treated by rubbing glycerine into the stain and leaving it for a while to loosen, then soaking the article in a solution of warm water and borax.

Older stains on carpets may require the use of a proprietary carpet-cleaning solution.

If you reach desperation and you think that the fabric can stand the heat, try pouring boiling water through the stain—this may shift the apparently impossible.

Cream

Marks made by cream spilled on washable garments will often come out completely if washed quickly enough, but in some cases a greasy mark may be left on the fabric. These marks can be removed with a dry-cleaning solution, dabbed on or, in aerosol form, lightly sprayed onto the area. Methylated spirit can also be useful in removing greasy marks left by cream, but you run risk of damaging the fabric if it is man-made. If you do choose to try methylated spirit, dilute a small amount with an equal quantity of water and see if you are successful with this before using it neat.

Greasy marks on carpets can be sponged with warm water and borax, or treated with dry-cleaning solution or carpet cleaner in aerosol form.

Curry

The spices used in cooking curry are responsible for some very stubborn stains. Scrape off any excess spillage, then gently dab a half-and-half solution of warm water and glycerine through the fabric, working from the wrong side. This should help to loosen the stain. Rinse in warm water, then wash, preferably using a biological powder. Stains on white cotton and linen should respond very well to soaking in a bleach solution, according to the bleach manufacturer's instructions.

Try treating non-washable items and carpets by dabbing with a solution of two tablespoons of borax and one litre of warm water. A more drastic alternative is to dab on a little methylated spirit, but try it diluted first, and carry out a spot-test on a spare piece of carpet first if possible.

Crayon

Crayon marks can be difficult to remove from fabrics. On fabrics that do not contain a high proportion of man-made fibres, dab a little methylated spirit onto the stain before washing and this may prove effective.

Marks made with wax crayon can also be treated with grease solvent or dry-cleaning fluid. You can try the iron and blotting paper method (see 'candle wax'), but this may still leave some of the colour behind. Methylated spirit may work on this.

Cycle Oil

If the mark is not too deeply embedded in the fabric, it may well come out if it is washed in the machine with a biological washing powder. Dabbing the fabric with soap prior to washing should help in the grease removal process. Soften the soap under warm water first, and this will make it easier to work it into the stain.

If the mark appears to be very deeply ingrained and is not fresh, pre-soaking the article in a borax solution might help, or you can try dabbing the stained area gently with methylated spirit prior to washing, providing that the fabric is suitable for such treatment.

Deodorant

Deodorants can leave an unpleasant scummy white mark on clothing, which can build up over a period of time in spite of washing. Mix up a paste of bicarbonate of soda and water and apply this to the marks, rubbing it in gently with your fingers. Leave this mixture on for half an hour or so, then soak the garment for a while in salty water. Rinse then wash as usual.

Dye Runs

Dye runs on white or very pale-coloured washable fabrics can be treated by soaking the garments in a weak solution of household bleach and water, according to the bleach manufacturer's instructions. There are products in the shops designed specifically to deal with the problem of dye runs, but if you are considering trying such a product, do check the suitability of the material for treatment before you make a purchase.

Egg

Egg stains on fabric should be soaked in a solution of detergent and water as soon as possible, and then washed, preferably with a biological washing powder. Do not use hot water for soaking; this will only cook the egg and make it more difficult to shift! If you have been unable to catch the stain while it is still fresh, use a solution of borax and water (two tablespoons of borax to one litre of water) for soaking the article.

Faeces

Unpleasant stains, but not too hard too remove. Scrape off any excess from the fabric, then soak, either in a solution of detergent and warm water, or borax and warm water (two tablespoons of borax to one litre of water) to loosen the stain. (If you have any nappy-soaking solution in the house you may be able to use this, but it is not really suitable for delicate materials.) Thereafter, wash the fabric in the usual manner, preferably using a biological powder and the hottest wash permissible for the fabric.

Carpets can also be treated with detergent or borax and warm water.

Fizzy Drinks

The food dyes that are used in the manufacture of some fizzy drinks can leave demon stains. When tackling stains on washable fabrics, rinse as much out as possible with lukewarm water, then dab the affected area with ammonia. Alternatively, try soaking the fabric in water with hydrogen peroxide; use 20 per cent volume hydrogen peroxide diluted with an equal quantity of water. Leave to soak for about fifteen minutes. White cottons can be soaked in bleach solution, according to the manufacturer's instructions.

Blot up excess spillage on carpets with kitchen roll, then work on the stain with warm water and white vinegar.

Fruit

Soft fruits are the main culprits here, and it is important to try to treat these stains as quickly as possible. On fabrics that can tolerate such harsh treatment, you can try pouring boiling water through the stain—simple but surprisingly effective! Fresh stains should respond to a brief soak in warm water and detergent, followed by a normal wash with a biological powder. If soaking does not appear to be shifting the stain, you can try dabbing lemon juice onto the area and leaving it for a while before washing.

If the fabric is unsuitable for soaking, dab it gently with a clean pad soaked in borax solution. If this proves unsuccessful, try dabbing it with white vinegar or lemon juice. Carpets can also be treated in this way. Rinse carefully after treatment.

On non-washable items, sponge off the worst with cold water and then either use a proprietary dry-cleaning product or take the article to be professionally cleaned.

If you have been picking or working with soft fruit and your hands have become stained, try rubbing them with lemon juice and salt before washing, and this should remove the unsightly marks.

Glue

There are very many different types of glue available in the shops, each with its own chemical make-up. If you have the container in which the glue was supplied in your possession, the first thing to do is to read the instructions carefully to see whether any advice is given on removal methods.

Luckily, many of the glues that are recommended for children's use are now washable. Do not, however, expect sizeable globules of glue to wash out of fabrics first time without some prior treatment. It is best to try to lift off as much as you can by hand; this can be quite tricky with looser woven or knitted fabrics. Then try to soften the glue with warm water and detergent, dabbing through gently from the reverse side of the fabric, before washing.

For non-washable glues, there may in fact be a

solvent available from the manufacturer; use as little as possible to minimize the risk of damage to the fabric. Where no proprietary solvent is available, you can try using methylated spirit, amyl acetate, or white spirit. Where drastic measures are required, you may try paintbrush cleaner or paint stripper, but there is great risk of damaging your material, so this really has to be a last resort.

Grass

Cotton fabrics can be safely treated by gently dabbing methylated spirit onto the stain. This treatment is not recommended for use on man-made fibres.

Fabrics requiring milder treatment should have a paste of detergent and warm water rubbed gently into the stain prior to soaking in detergent solution. Thereafter, rinse and wash in the usual manner. Fabrics with any sort of special finish are best sent for dry-cleaning.

Treat grass stains as soon as possible in order to maximize your chances of removing them.

Gravy

Most gravy stains can be removed from washable fabrics by pre-soaking the article in detergent and water solution, then washing it using a good biological washing powder.

Non-washable fabrics should be sponged gently with lukewarm water and detergent; this may well leave a grease stain still to be removed (see below).

Grease

Lift off any excess gently, using the blunt edge of a knife. Talcum powder or fuller's earth, sprinkled onto the area and left for a while, should help to absorb the grease. On washable fabrics, soften some soap under warm water and rub this gently into the mark before washing, preferably with a biological washing powder. Eucalyptus oil is an alternative to this. Rubbed into a greasy stain, it will help break down the grease before washing.

It is more difficult to wash grease stains out of carpets without over-wetting them. You can use fuller's earth or talcum powder and then vacuum it off, then once the excess has been absorbed, you can try sponging it with borax and warm water, then rinsing carefully with repeated small amounts of water. On large stains, however, it is probably advisable to use a proprietary carpet cleaner.

Methylated spirit can be used on grease marks, but there is a risk of fading the colour, or, on some man-made fabrics, of damaging the fabric itself. Try using it diluted with water first; only if that fails should you resort to using it neat. If you have a sample of fabric or carpet on which you can carry out a spot-test, it is advisable to do this before you use something as strong as methylated spirits.

Dry-clean-only fabrics can be treated gently with methylated spirit, but you are probably safer to use a dry-cleaning aerosol, or to take the article for professional cleaning.

Hair Spray

Hair spray can stain clothing if used carelessly, but a gentle sponging with borax solution is usually enough to remove the mark. It can also leave a sticky mess on mirrors, but this should come off with hot water and vinegar.

Ice Cream

Most ice-cream stains will come out of fabric easily using normal washing methods and a good washing powder. Stains on carpets can be gently sponged with warm water and detergent and, providing the stain has not dried in, they should come out without any problem.

However, some fruit-juice-based mixtures may cause more staining; blackcurrant sorbet, for example, can be more than a little bit tricky! Rinse the fabric thoroughly with cold water without delay, then leave it to soak for a while in a solution of warm water and biological washing powder. Try treating persistent stains with lemon juice before re-washing.

Ink—Ballpoint Pen

Inks that are used in ballpoint pens vary, so it is safest to start with soap and water when treating a ballpoint stain. Ordinary hand soap, softened under warm water and then pressed gently through the material, can help to shift the stain before rinsing. Make sure that the water that you use is neither too hot nor too cold to avoid the risk of setting the stain.

If this is unsuccessful, try dabbing hot milk through the stain, or stretching the stained part of the fabric over a beaker and pouring the hot milk through it. Do not use the hot-milk treatment on wool, as you could cause matting and shrinkage. Neither is this treatment recommended for carpets—unless you can be absolutely sure of being able to rinse the milk out properly, you will be left with a most unpleasant smell!

Methylated spirit is a last resort. It can certainly shift the stain fairly quickly, but it may prove to be equally good at removing some of the colour from the fabric! If you are treating man-made fabric, it is safest to dilute the methylated spirit, one part spirit to two parts water, to minimize the risk of damage to the material. If you have no methylated spirit, you can try dabbing a little white spirit onto the stain.

Ink—Felt-tip Pen

Many felt-tip pens, especially those produced for the children's market, are washable. Marks left by such pens should respond quite readily to a soak in a solution of detergent and warm water, followed by a wash with biological powder.

If you are unsure as to whether the pen that made the mark is washable or not, you may like to try treating the mark either by dabbing it with methylated spirit, applied with a clean white pad of fabric, or by treating it with a dry-cleaning solution, according to the manufacturer's instructions. However, it is important that you ensure that the fabric that you are treating is unlikely to be damaged by the use of these substances. Red ink is notoriously more difficult to remove than others; you may have to resort to using methylated spirit where this is the culprit. The only time to despair, however, is if the stain has been made by permanent marker pen. Removal will probably be impossible; opting for camouflage instead is probably a better course of action.

Ink—Fountain Pen

Many brands of ink for fountain pens are washable nowadays. On carpets, or fabrics where a large quantity of ink has been spilt, pour some salt onto the stain while it is wet and leave it until it has soaked up the ink. Then brush the salt off carefully, making sure that you do not rub any of it back into the fabric in the process. Thereafter, wash fabrics on the hottest wash permissible. Carpets can be dabbed with a half-and-half mixture of white vinegar and warm water.

If the treatments above do not work, then you may like to try the treatments that have been recommended for ballpoint pen stains or to try using one of the stain-specific cleaning solutions that are available in the shops.

Although it is perhaps safe to say that most fountain pen inks are removable, Indian ink may well not be possible to remove.

Jam

On washable items, scrape off any excess with the blunt edge off a knife and then sponge the article with warm water and liquid detergent. Then wash the article as normal.

Marks on carpets can also be treated with detergent and warm water. Take care not to overwet the area, and rinse off the detergent carefully.

Slight marks on dry-cleanable items may come out if you sponge them very gently with warm water. Otherwise, use a proprietary dry-cleaning product or take the article to be cleaned professionally.

Ketchup

If you catch stains made by tomato ketchup quickly enough, you should be able to treat them by dabbing them with warm water and detergent. Washable items can be soaked for a while in water and detergent prior to washing.

Treat older stains by rubbing glycerine into the material to loosen the stain and leaving it for a while before soaking and washing, or simply washing, Use a biological washing powder for washing, preferably.

Sponge non-washable items and carpets with

water and borax, or use a proprietary cleaning product.

Lipstick

Lipstick is first and foremost a greasy stain; treat the grease first. Dab it gently with either washing-up liquid or softened toilet soap. This should loosen the grease before washing. Alternatively, you can apply a little eucalyptus oil to break down the grease. If you are left with some colour staining after washing, you may try a little white spirit on the mark, or, on white cotton fabrics, you can try bleach, diluted with cold water according to the manufacturer's instructions.

Non-washable fabrics should be taken to the dry-cleaner's as quickly as possible.

Make-up

Make-up other than lipstick is usually quite straightforward to remove from washable fabrics. Sponge with softened soap and warm water, then wash as normal.

On non-washable articles, small marks can be treated by gently sponging them with warm soapy water. Otherwise, it is best to use a suitable dry-cleaning product, or to take the article for professional cleaning.

Mildew

Mildew is quite difficult to remove, but there are a few alternative ways of treating it. White washable fabrics may well respond successfully to soaking in bleach solution before washing. Coloured fabrics can be rubbed gently with a paste made from salt and a little water, then soaked in salty water before washing. Another option is to soak the fabric in a weak solution of hydrogen peroxide before washing. Dilute 20 per cent volume strength hydrogen peroxide with an equal amount of water and use this.

Mildew on carpets is probably best left to the experts; unless it is successfully removed, it will only spread. Mildew thrives in damp conditions; thus it can be found in places such as poorly-ventilated bathrooms. Unless the cause of the mildew forming on your carpets, i.e. the damp conditions, are attended to, the problem will only repeat itself.

Mildew on paintwork and tile grout may be removed with a bleach solution, or by using a mildew-removing product, available from any DIY store or ironmonger's.

Milk

Milk generally does not cause a problem stain unless it is particularly creamy. Most milk stains can be removed very easily by either sponging them with warm water and detergent or giving the article a brief soak in water and detergent before washing. If the stain looks greasy, you can, if you wish, dab it with a little dilute methylated spirit.

The problem with milk is that spillages on carpets can leave an unpleasant lingering smell. Try to be as sure as you possibly can that all trace of the milk has been removed and that the area has been well rinsed. Carpets should be rinsed with repeated applications of small amounts of water. Blot up the water in between rinses to avoid the area becoming over-wet.

Mud

Unlike most other stains, which are best treated immediately, mud stains are best left to dry. Most of the mud can then be gently brushed out of the material. The material can then be washed as normal. Dry-clean-only fabrics can be dabbed gently with a little warm water; unless there is a great amount of soiling, this should be enough to remove the mark, thereby avoiding the necessity for expensive cleaning bills.

Mud on carpets can be left to dry and then removed with a vacuum cleaner.

Nail Varnish

Nail varnish remover will be effective in shifting nail varnish from some fabrics, but the acetone in this product will damage fabrics that contain acetate. If you are at all unsure of the fibre content of the fabric that you are treating, use amyl acetate instead. Amyl acetate should be available from your chemist. Spot-test the fabric first, if possible, for colour fading. If you are at all worried that the colour of the fabric might fade, take the garment to a specialist dry-cleaner instead.

There may be some colour staining left after the varnish is removed; treat this cautiously with diluted methylated spirit.

Nail varnish that has been spilt on a non-absorbent surface such as a vinyl floor should be left to dry and then gently peeled off.

Nicotine

If there is a smoker in your house, curtains will have to be washed or dry-cleaned regularly to keep them fresh and free of nicotine stains. Unless they are cleaned regularly, a build-up of nicotine staining is inevitable, collecting especially around the pleats at the top, and there will be little you can do to restore the curtains to their proper colours. Unless the smoking can be stopped, choosing darker colours for your curtain fabrics is the best means of disguising the staining, although regular cleaning will still be necessary to keep the curtains smelling fresh.

Staining on washable walls and wallpapers can be treated with a solution of sugar soap and water; this will do much to improve matters. Unfortunately on non-washable wallpapers there is little you can do.

If you cannot declare the area a smoke-free zone, you will simply have to put up with unpleasantly yellowing walls.

Nicotine stains on fingers can be removed by rubbing them with lemon juice before washing with soap and water.

Paint—Acrylic

Acrylic paint will come out of fabrics and carpets without any problem if you catch it while it is wet. You need only use cold water and it should rinse out quite easily. It may be possible to pick hardened acrylic paint off fabrics, but failing that, you may have to resort to paintbrush cleaning fluid and risk damaging the fabric.

Paint—Emulsion

Emulsion paint is a classic example of a stain that can be removed easily when fresh. Unfortunately, it is well-nigh impossible to get out once the paint has dried!

While the paint is still wet, sponge the affected area of fabric as generously as you dare with warm water. Work from the reverse side of the fabric if possible, trying to push the stain back out. Then work on the stain using warm water and a generous quantity of detergent. When you are confident that the stain is almost out, rinse thoroughly then wash in the usual manner.

Carpets should be treated with detergent and water, but care must be taken not to over-wet the area.

Older stains are really tricky; you can try paintbrush cleaning solution, but this can be very dangerous to all but the most hardy of fabrics.

Paint—Oil-Based Gloss and Enamel

These stains are best caught fresh. Whenever you are decorating at home, or using gloss or enamel paint for any project, have a bottle of white spirit or turpentine and some clean rags to hand. You are sure to need them!

Dab the affected area with a clean pad of fabric dipped in white spirit or turpentine. Use as little spirit as possible in order to remove the stain without damaging the fabric.

Dry gloss paint can be treated with paintbrush cleaner, but this is a very strong solvent, and it is used only at great risk to the fabric being treated.

Great care should be used with white spirit, turpentine and paintbrush cleaner. Never smoke when you are using them, and keep the area in which you are working well ventilated.

Paint—Poster

Poster paint is generally thought to be washable, but sometimes some colours, red in particular, can leave a stain. You can try treating washable items with hydrogen peroxide solution, 20 per cent volume strength, diluted with the same quantity of water. Leave the article in this solution for about fifteen minutes and then wash as usual.

Spot-test this solution on coloured articles before use.

Perspiration

Perspiration marks on white cotton garments can be shifted by soaking in a bleach solution, according to the manufacturer's instructions. Alternatively, you can try dabbing the marks with ammonia, white vinegar or lemon juice. Rinse out, then wash as normal.

Rust

Lemon juice and salt are your best allies when trying to remove rust marks from articles of clothing. Saturate the stain with the lemon juice, then sprinkle on a generous amount of salt. Leave this to work on the stain for a short while; if you can spread it out in the sunlight, so much the better. Thereafter, rinse out the article and wash as normal.

Rust marks on carpets are best treated with proprietary carpet-cleaning products, but if the mark is only a slight one, it may come out with lemon juice diluted with water.

Scorch Marks

Severe scorching is, unfortunately, probably there to stay, but light scorching can be treated with a half-and-half water and hydrogen peroxide solution dabbed gently onto the fabric. Alternatively, you can try dabbing on a borax solution, or, on suitable fabrics, soaking in bleach solution. After treatment, rinse then wash as normal.

Shoe Polish

Shoe polish can be treated much in the same way as many other greasy stains, such as cycle oil, but you will probably find it hard to remove the colour staining. White spirit or methylated spirit may prove effective but should be used with caution; the colour of the fabric could be altered, and in some cases the fabric could be damaged. Dry-cleaning aerosol sprays can give success but must be used with care.

Tar

Tar stains on clothing can be quite a problem for holiday-makers who have visited the beach, but they are easily treatable. Oil of eucalyptus, which should be available from any good pharmacist, will prove quite effective. Lift off any excess tar with the blunt edge of a kitchen knife, then treat the stain from the reverse of the fabric, dabbing the eucalyptus oil into the fibres to push the tar back out. Following treatment, rinse and wash as normal.

Dry-clean-only fabrics can also be treated with eucalyptus oil before being taken for cleaning, but it is advisable to let the cleaner know that you have done this when you hand it over.

Tea

Tea stains should not be a problem on washable fabrics, if they are treated without delay. Soak the garment or cloth in warm water and detergent, preferably overnight, then wash as normal. Older stains can be soaked overnight in borax solution before washing. Alternatively, dab glycerine onto the fabric, working it into the fibres. Leave this for a while to loosen the stain before washing.

If the fabric is suitable for the hottest wash in the washing machine, this may well be all that is required to remove tea stains.

Non-washable fabrics can be treated with dry-cleaning aerosol (used with caution) or dabbed with a clean pad soaked in borax solution. If you prefer to have the article dry-cleaned, then it should be treated at the earliest opportunity.

Tea stains on carpets must be caught quickly. Soak up excess liquid with kitchen towels, then sponge with water and detergent, or borax solution.

Urine

Urine, whether animal or human, can leave an unpleasant stain and an offensive smell.

Fresh urine staining on clothing can be treated simply by rinsing the article thoroughly in cold water and then washing it as normal, preferably using a biological washing powder.

Clothing with older, dried-in urine staining should be soaked overnight in a weak solution of hydrogen peroxide and water before washing. If you have no hydrogen peroxide available, soak the article in salty water instead, then wash.

Urine stains on carpets should be sponged with salty water after the excess urine has been soaked up with paper kitchen towels. If you have a soda siphon, soda water squirted onto the urine-soaked area is an alternative way to prevent staining.

The smell of urine may linger on the carpet if the puddle has not been cleaned up in time. Once you are sure that the area is clean, sprinkle on some bicarbonate of soda and leave for a while to dry before brushing it off or removing it with a vacuum cleaner. When you have brushed off the bicarbonate of soda, you should notice an improvement in the smell.

Vomit

Vomit stains can be easy to remove or can prove quite stubborn, depending on what has been consumed before vomiting! Always clean up vomit as quickly as possible, especially on carpets and mattresses, where as little as possible should be allowed to soak in. Lift or scrape up all solid matter and blot up any excess fluid with paper kitchen towels. Articles of clothing should then be rinsed thoroughly in water, then washed with a biological washing powder. If the vomit is known to contain something particularly staining, such as wine, then it is advisable to leave the article to soak for a while in salty water. If the vomit appears to be particularly greasy, you can soak the article for a short while in borax solution, using two tablespoons of borax to one litre of water. Carpets should be sponged with warm water to which detergent suitable for washing woollens or hand-wash garments has been added, or warm water and borax solution, and then rinsed thoroughly.

Any unpleasant smell that lingers after cleaning has been completed should disappear if you sprinkle bicarbonate of soda on the affected area, leave it for a while, and then remove it with a brush or a vacuum cleaner.

Wine

White wine does not present a problem as regards stains; any spillages can be simply blotted up and sponged off with soapy water.

Red wine, especially the darker varieties, can leave a very ugly purple-blue stain if not treated correctly.

Fresh red wine stains can be treated very successfully with white wine if you can afford it; simply pour the white wine onto the stain, wait a couple of moments, and then rinse it away; the red wine marks will disappear as you do so. This method is equally as successful for red wine spillages on carpets as it is on fabrics, but you have to be careful not to pour on too much white wine; apart from the fact that this would be very wasteful, it would leave the carpet very wet and could cause shrinkage.

For those of you who are not in the habit of having a spare bottle of white wine to hand, or who do not like the thought of good wine being frittered away in such a manner, the alternative, salt, is almost as effective and certainly cheaper.

Pour enough salt onto the spillage to cover the area completely. As the wine soaks up into the salt, add some more. Keep adding salt until it stops absorbing the wine. Some advocates of this method would recommend sweeping up the salt immediately, but it is better to leave it until the salt is drier, thus avoiding pushing any of the wine back into the fabric as you sweep the salt up.

A third option for treating red wine stains is to soak them in soda water, but this does not guarantee success.

Wine stains that have been left to dry are more of a problem. If all else fails, and you think that the fabric can stand up to it, pour boiling water through the stain and you may finally have some success.

Store Cupboard Items for Stain Removal

There are a few items that you should consider keeping in stock, which can help you to cope with unexpected stains.

1] Ammonia

Ammonia is a useful household cleaning and bleaching agent. Many household cleaners contain ammonia. It has a very strong smell and its fumes can be quite unpleasant, so always keep the area in which you are working with it very well ventilated.

Always use it in dilute form, at least five parts of water to each of ammonia.

Ammonia can cause burns and adverse skin reactions, so it is advisable to wear rubber gloves when using it. It is not suitable for use on woollen or silk-based fabrics.

2] Amyl Acetate

Amyl acetate should be available from good chemists. It is safer to use than nail varnish remover, which contains acetone and can damage acetate fibres.

Amyl acetate will be effective in removing nail varnish from fabric and can successfully remove some kinds of glue. It does, however, carry with it some risk of fading the colour on the fabric you are treating; if possible, carry out a spot-test first]to minimize this risk.

3] Bleach

Household bleach is always a good stand-by for the treatment of white cottons and linens that have become discoloured or stained but is not suitable for use on many other fabrics and should not be used on silk or wool. Always follow the manufacturer's instructions carefully when using bleach; never use it undiluted. Household bleach contains chlorine, and you should never use it in conjunction with any other cleaning products as the chemicals in the cleaning products could react with the chlorine and give off toxic fumes. After soaking articles in bleach solution, always rinse them very thoroughly before washing.

4] Borax

Borax is a compound of boracic acid and soda and is available in powder or crystal form from chemists and some supermarkets. It has several uses in stain-removing. It should be used in solution, two tablespoons of borax per litre of water, for soaking or sponging stains. It has a mild bleaching effect, so do not leave articles to soak in borax solution for longer than about fifteen minutes.

5] Clean, White, Absorbent Rags

Old towels, torn-up bits of flannelette sheets, and old terry nappies are perfect for this. You can use them for dabbing cleaning solution or water onto stains, or for placing under stained fabric while you work on it from the other side. White rags are best; there is no risk of leaving any further staining from fabric dye as you work, and you can see against the white material just how much of the stain you are removing.

6] Glycerine

Glycerine has its culinary uses, but it is also an invaluable part of any good stain-removal kit. It can work its magic on quite a few old stains if it is rubbed in and left for a little while. It is particularly effective when used on old bloodstains.

7] Hydrogen Peroxide

Hydrogen peroxide is usually available in 20 per cent volume strength from chemists. It has bleaching and disinfecting properties but is not as strong as household bleach. It is safe for use on wool and silk, but should never be used on nylon. Dilute hydrogen peroxide before use, with at least six times its volume of water, and do not soak articles in the solution for longer than fifteen minutes or you risk colour fading.

In very dilute form, hydrogen peroxide can be dabbed onto scorch marks on fabric to remove them.

8] Lemon Juice

Lemon juice and salt are a great combination for removing some stains. Lemon juice, rubbed into your hands after peeling onions or garlic, is also useful as a deodorizer.

9] Methylated Spirit

Methylated spirit can be quite a powerful weapon to use in the war against stains, but it does carry risks. It is volatile and flammable and should be stored and used with great care. It can remove dye in some fabrics, and can damage the fabric itself if it contains acetate fibres. Dilute it with twice its volume of water rather than using it undiluted unless the stain you are treating is proving to be especially stubborn.

10] Oil of Eucalyptus

Apart from having quite a pleasant smell, oil of eucalyptus, which you should be able to obtain from a good chemist or ironmonger, is very handy for breaking down particularly greasy stains, such as tar.

11] Paper Kitchen Roll

Kitchen roll is more than worth its weight in gold. Its absorbent qualities are unbeatable for soaking up spillages.

12] Salt

Salty water is surprisingly effective in the treatment of some stains, and unbeatable when removing fresh blood staining. Always keep a spare bag of table salt in stock; you may need it to deal with a wine spillage, and you will find that you need to use quite a lot.

13] White Spirit

When you are decorating or using gloss or enamel paint for some project, the white spirit should always be to hand. Use white spirit carefully, however, for it is highly flammable and its fumes are quite unpleasant.

14] White Vinegar

A drop or two of vinegar in warm water can be quite effective against some stains, and it is a cheap and harmless thing to use. Vinegar is also useful for cleaning windows; use it in your cleaning water instead of detergent and you will have fewer problems getting a smear-free finish.

In addition to the above, you will probably find it useful to keep in stock some dry cleaning fluid or aerosol spray and a can of spot remover for carpets and upholstery.